P9-CAD-046

# QUICKSAND

## HIV/AIDS IN OUR LIVES

# QUICKSAND

## HIV/AIDS IN OUR LIVES

**ANONYMOUS**

CANDLEWICK PRESS

First edition 2009

Library of Congress Cataloging-in-Publication Data

Quicksand : HIV/AIDS in our lives /
by Anonymous. —1st ed.
p. cm.
Includes bibliographical references and index.
ISBN 978-0-7636-1589-5
1. AIDS (Disease)— Patients — Mental health.
2. AIDS (Disease)—Transmission. 3. AIDS phobia.
I. Title.
RC606.6Q45 2009
616.97'90 — dc22     2009007761

09 10 11 12 13 14 WCF 10 9 8 7 6 5 4 3 2 1

Printed in the Fairfield, PA, U.S.A.

This book was typeset in Giovanni.

Candlewick Press
99 Dover Street
Somerville, Massachusetts 02144

visit us at www.candlewick.com

*For all the people who have quietly battled
HIV/AIDS, especially Jay and Nan,
and those who have stood by them in
their hidden world*

*For privacy reasons, all the names in this book
have been changed except for those already
in the public record.*

# CONTENTS

# Why I Wrote This Book

The Still Hidden World of HIV/AIDS
in America

The reason I can't put my name on this book is the reason I knew I had to write it. One day, more than ten years ago, I found out that someone I know—my brother-in-law, Jay—had HIV/AIDS.

You may think a lot has changed since that time. In fact, you may even think that AIDS isn't a big deal in America anymore. But even though there have been medical advancements in treating this condition, people continue to be diagnosed with HIV/AIDS every day. And even though, thanks to efforts by activists and educators, HIV/AIDS is discussed more openly now, many people still feel uncomfortable, fearful, or judgmental around people with HIV/AIDS. Because of this, many people with HIV/AIDS still choose to keep their condition a secret.

While I would prefer to be open about my identity, both Jay and his mother asked me to keep it a secret, too. This means that in order to keep my promise to them and to respect and protect their privacy, I can't tell you who I am. I am remaining anonymous rather than using a fake name because I want you to realize that I am only one of perhaps millions of people in America and all over the world who are hiding the fact that someone in their lives has HIV/AIDS.

Because HIV/AIDS is not always discussed openly, it can be tough to get answers to questions that occur when you learn that someone you know has HIV/AIDS. I've tried to answer as many of those questions as I can in this book. I've also told some of Jay's story, even though, thanks to medical research, many aspects of his treatment are now out-of-date. While the story of his battle with AIDS describes just one person's experience, it is a true story, and one that shows how the needless secrecy and fear about HIV/AIDS can keep people isolated. It is my hope that his story will inspire compassion for those who do not feel able to be vocal about their HIV status, respect for those who are brave enough to speak openly about this disease, and determination to change the world so that one day, no person with HIV/AIDS will have to hide it ever again.

. . . . . . . . . . . . . . . . . . . . . . . . . . . . . . . . . . . . . . . . . . . . . . . . . . . .

## What is HIV?

HIV is the acronym (an abbreviation made up of the first letters of the words in a phrase) for the scientific term *human immunodeficiency virus*. It's called *human* because it affects people. *Immunodeficiency* means that the immune system is weakened or, in other words, not able to fight off infections. *Virus* is the word for a particular type of germ.

HIV is sometimes called the AIDS virus because HIV is the virus that can lead to AIDS. There are actually a number of different strains, or slight variations, of HIV. They all cause AIDS. For simplicity's sake, I will use the term HIV to cover all of these strains throughout this book.

HIV affects the body by attacking white cells called T cells. These helper cells protect the body from dangerous germs including bacteria, parasites, and certain viruses, but unfortunately, T cells cannot kill HIV and are instead themselves destroyed by this virus. Left unchecked, HIV keeps replicating, or copying itself, over time so that there is more and more of the virus present in the system and fewer and fewer T cells.

## T Cells

T cells are a certain type of white blood cell that is very important to the immune system. They are called T cells because they spend time in the thymus, a gland in the upper chest.

T cells are formed in the bone marrow. They migrate to the thymus, where they mature. Then they spread throughout the body, where they attack and kill invading germs. HIV infects and destroys T cells. Without enough T cells, the immune system eventually weakens and shuts down.

There are two main types of T cells. One is CD4 cells, which lead the attack against infections. The other is CD8 cells, which end the immune response and kill cancer cells and those infected with a virus.

When HIV infects people, the cells it infects most are CD4 cells. The virus becomes part of these cells. When they multiply to fight an infection, they also make more copies of HIV.

# What is AIDS?

AIDS is the acronym for the scientific term *acquired immune deficiency syndrome. Acquired* is the word for something that you can get. *Immune* refers to the immune system, the system of cells and organs that fight off infections in the body. *Deficiency* means not having enough, and *syndrome* refers to the collection of diseases brought on by HIV infection.

When the number of CD4 cells falls too low in an HIV-infected person, his or her body can usually no longer fight other germs effectively. Then that person becomes sick with the opportunistic infections — infections such as tuberculosis that take advantage of a weakened immune system — that are associated with AIDS. If a person has a CD4 cell count of less than 200, doctors then say that he or she has AIDS. There are some HIV-positive people with a CD4 cell count of less than 200 who feel relatively well for a while. Other people with the virus have a count of more than 200 but they have AIDS-related symptoms. The definition of AIDS includes either CD4 cell counts or symptoms or both of these.

## How did HIV/AIDS start?

No one knows exactly how HIV began. Researchers have data that suggest there was cross-species transmission from chimpanzees to humans of a virus during the twentieth century, probably from chimpanzees being killed and eaten or from chimpanzee blood coming into contact with cuts in the skin of hunters.

No one knows who the first HIV-infected person was, but HIV has been traced to an unidentified man who gave a blood sample in Kinshasa, then called Léopoldville, in 1959. This was in an area that is now called the Congo.

The first cases of the AIDS epidemic in the United States were reported in 1981. They were primarily in the gay male community. However, worldwide, cases were more widespread. Eventually, HIV/AIDS was discovered in the general population in America, too. Now people of all ages and both sexes have HIV/AIDS. It has become a global pandemic.

In the beginning, AIDS was considered fatal because there was no way to treat it. While there is still no cure, thanks to medical research and improved treatments, that is no longer the case.

# How many people have HIV/AIDS now?

Worldwide, HIV/AIDS is extremely widespread. As of 2007, about 33 million people have it. Picture New York City in your mind. New York City has about 8 million people, so more than four times that many people are afflicted. Each one of them probably has at least ten people who care about them, including family, friends, and/or medical workers. This would mean that more than 330 million of us are currently being directly affected in one way or another by HIV/AIDS. As of 2007, the estimated number of Americans living with HIV/AIDS was 1.2 million. More than 250,000 of them may be unaware that they are infected. More than 420,000 Americans are living with AIDS, and there are more than 55,000 new HIV infections in the United States every year.

Because this book is based on my personal experience, it doesn't talk about AIDS in countries outside of North America. However, in many parts of the world, particularly sub-Saharan Africa, HIV/AIDS is very common, and issues of prevention and treatment have become critical. If you want to learn more about this crisis, please see the websites listed at the end of this book.

# Quicksand

Jay's Diagnosis

More than ten years ago, in 1995, my husband and I paid our usual summer visit to his family. My brother-in-law, Jay, was coughing constantly during our stay. He was taking antibiotics for bronchitis, but his condition had been worsening and he had lost a lot of weight. We were very concerned about Jay's health.

A few weeks later, my husband's mother called one night to say that Jay was having trouble breathing. She planned to take him to the doctor the next morning.

My husband and I became alarmed. We pulled a medical reference book from our bookshelf and read the symptoms of pneumonia to my husband's mother over the phone. When we reached the part that said to call your doctor if the sharp chest pain and shortness of breath does not respond to the prescribed treatment and if the fingernails have a bluish tinge, she decided to take him to the emergency room at a nearby hospital right away.

That evening Jay was in such poor shape that the doctor had to begin treating him even before there was a diagnosis, since the results of all the tests would not be ready for a few days. The doctor decided to give Jay antibiotics for a type of lung infection that is found in patients whose immune systems are severely run down.

Jay had been a smoker for thirty-three years — since he was thirteen — so we were afraid that he had lung cancer. We did not know then that Jay had also engaged in other risky behaviors such as injecting drugs and having unprotected sex, so we were unaware of what other medical conditions he could have been facing.

The doctor warned us that Jay might not survive the night. However, by the next morning, he was still clinging to life. My husband and I drove down to visit him at the hospital. Before we walked into Jay's room, we were given

# Germs and Viruses

A germ is a microbe or tiny organism that can cause disease. Germs are so small that they can be seen only through a microscope.

Viruses are one kind of germ. Because they do not have the structure of cells, they are not considered living organisms. To grow and multiply, a virus must invade a living organism — a plant or an animal.

There are many different kinds of viruses, and not all viruses are deadly. For instance, a common cold is caused by any one of more than 200 viruses that infect the nose and throat.

Communicable germs can be passed from one person to another. There are three basic ways this can happen.

First, some are spread through direct contact with the body fluids of infected people.

Second, some are caught by touching objects an infected person has used.

Third, some are transmitted by insects and other animals.

HIV is spread only the first way — in some situations involving direct contact with certain body fluids of infected people.

surgical masks and gloves to wear. He was in an oxygen tent and being kept away from the other patients in case his disease was a contagious one such as tuberculosis.

A few days later, we found out what was wrong. Jay called us to say that an HIV test they had given him was positive. This meant he was infected with HIV.

At the time we didn't know too much about HIV/AIDS, but we tried to be as encouraging as we could. My husband reminded Jay that lots of people are HIV-positive and remain healthy for years. Not long after the HIV test results came, though, the diagnosis for Jay's lung infection was made. He had *pneumocystis* pneumonia (PCP). At that time in the epidemic, PCP was often found in AIDS patients whose immune systems were exhausted. Jay was so sick that he already had AIDS. PCP itself was not considered a life-threatening illness if treated. However, in the mid-1990s — unlike today — AIDS was a death sentence.

The doctors gave Jay less than six months to live.

We were devastated.

Like millions before us, we had stepped into the quicksand of a new and terrible world and we were sinking fast. The long ordeal for Jay and our family had begun.

· · · · · · · · · · · · · · · · · · · · · · · · · · · · · · · · · · · · · · · · · · ·

## How can you tell if someone has HIV?

The answer is very simple. You can't.

After getting HIV, an infected person can look and seem healthy for a long time. But even though they feel well, they can transmit the virus.

The only real way to know whether someone has the virus that leads to AIDS is if he or she takes an HIV test.

## How are people tested for HIV?

There are a number of ways. The two main types of tests look for HIV antibodies in either an oral or blood sample. The newer versions of these tests take about twenty minutes to find out the results, depending on the laboratory involved.

If the test results are positive, the person has HIV. Then we say that the person is HIV-positive.

If the test results are negative, the person does not have this virus. The person is HIV-negative.

## HIV Tests

HIV tests determine whether someone has been infected with HIV. When someone has HIV, antibodies begin to form in his or her body. These are proteins produced in response to HIV. It usually takes two to twelve weeks after infection for antibodies to HIV to develop.

The time between infection and the presence of antibodies to HIV is called the window period. If someone who is infected is tested during this window period, the antibodies to HIV may not have appeared yet. This means that even though the person has HIV, the test will not show it.

Whenever the medical staff determines that a person might have been tested during a window period, it is routine to use alternative tests or to repeat the tests to identify HIV infection.

## Are HIV tests always accurate?

Most of the time they are. However, no test is 100 percent accurate. Every now and then, there could be a false positive test result for reasons that are not clearly understood.

There might be a false negative test result as well. This might happen because the HIV infection is too recent for a test to pick up the presence of antibodies.

This is why the Centers for Disease Control and Prevention (CDC) recommend that someone be retested with a second newly collected specimen to confirm his or her HIV-positive or HIV-negative status.

## How do people get HIV?

HIV is spread in four different ways: direct contact with blood, sexual contact, and from mother to child during pregnancy or breast-feeding. These are discussed in the questions that follow.

## How do people get HIV through blood?

If people have HIV, it is found in high enough levels in their blood to cause it to be infectious. If someone who doesn't have HIV comes into direct contact with HIV-infected blood, he or she could catch the virus, too. This might happen if he or she had a cut or open sore in his or her skin and touched HIV-infected blood. This is called blood-to-blood contact. HIV can also be transmitted from infected blood to mucous membranes such as those of the eyes, nose, and mouth. This is called blood-to-membrane contact.

This is why you *always* need to use a set of procedures called Standard Precautions in *any* situations involving blood. This includes dried blood. Such blood may contain other disease-causing germs, even if the HIV has already been destroyed when the blood dried out.

## What are Standard Precautions?

Standard Precautions are a set of procedures that hospitals and other medical settings use to prevent the spread of disease-causing germs from one person to another. They were developed by the CDC to protect both patients and medical workers from infecting each other. They are called standard because they are routine; they are used at all times whether or not a person has been diagnosed with an infectious disease.

Some examples of the personal protective equipment involved are barriers such as gloves, gowns, eye protectors, and masks. All health-care workers wear them to protect against direct contact with any patient's blood, body fluids, secretions, excretions (except sweat), mucous membranes, or non-intact skin.

For the purposes of this book, we will refer only to those aspects of Standard Precautions that are needed in ordinary life situations, such as using latex or plastic gloves to prevent the spread of HIV in all situations where blood is present, whether or not you know the person has HIV.

## Can you get HIV/AIDS from a needle or syringe?

Yes, it is possible to transmit HIV if two people use the same needle after each other. Some people who use illegal or legal drugs outside of a doctor's office share needles and syringes with one another. When injecting these drugs, a tiny amount of blood can remain in the needle.

If the needle is used again, then this blood can enter the second needle user's bloodstream. If the blood is infected with HIV, the second needle user could get the virus. It only takes the amount of blood in a pinprick to pass HIV on to someone else.

Many communities with a known population of people using injected drugs hand out disposable needles. These needles are used only once and then discarded to prevent the spread of HIV.

## Can you get HIV from a shot at the doctor's office?

No. In medical settings in the United States, Standard Precautions are used, including disposable needles. Your doctor will never use the same needle on two different patients, so you are safe.

## Can you get HIV/AIDS from going to the dentist?

No. Dentists in America use Standard Precautions in their work. They sterilize their dental tools and use disposable needles and syringes. So you shouldn't be afraid that someone else's blood could contaminate you at a dentist's office.

## If you get a tattoo or your ears or body pierced, can you get HIV?

Yes. If you have these things done at an unlicensed place that reuses needles, you could get HIV, since small amounts of blood may remain on the needle between uses. It is important that disposable needles always be used. Before you let anyone do any tattooing or body piercing, make sure that the studio has a current license and inspection issued by the health department in your state. You can find such places by looking in the phone book or by contacting your state health department.

Sometimes people allow friends or strangers to pierce their ears or bodies for them at home or at parties or other settings. This is never a good idea. They could be at a high risk of getting HIV this way.

## Can you get this virus from sharing a razor or toothbrush?

Yes, it is possible to get HIV this way, though it is very unlikely. Nevertheless, you should never share anyone's razor. If even a tiny amount of blood remains on it and you cut yourself while shaving, you might get HIV and/or other blood-borne germs into your own bloodstream.

It's not a good idea to share anyone's toothbrush, either. Sometimes people's gums bleed when they brush their teeth, and contact with blood can spread HIV or other germs.

## Can you get HIV from a blood transfusion?

Most likely, no. At one time, some people did get HIV from blood transfusions, but now the blood supply is screened for HIV, so it is much safer. But the risk of receiving HIV-infected blood will never be zero because people who don't realize that they have HIV might donate blood during the window period, when HIV cannot yet be detected.

Sometimes people know in advance that they are going to have an operation. At some hospitals, they can give some of their own blood before the operation to use in case it is needed.

# How do people get HIV during sex?

If someone has HIV, it is present in his or her sexual secretions. If a man has HIV, it's found in his semen and other sexual fluids. If a woman has HIV, it's found in her vaginal fluids, including menstrual blood. If either of them has sex with someone else, they can transmit HIV to their partner through fluid to membrane contact. Anyone, male or female, can get and spread HIV during sex.

Abstinence is the only way to eliminate the risk of getting HIV through sex. Abstinence means not having any oral, anal, or vaginal sex. Many people assume that oral sex is not risky because it will not cause pregnancy. However, although HIV transmission through oral sex is rare, there is still some risk. People can also get other sexually transmitted diseases (STDs) from oral, anal, or vaginal sex.

If you are having sexual experiences, you can significantly reduce these risks by using protection. This includes knowing how to find and use a new latex or polyurethane condom with a water-based lubricant each time you have sex. Used properly, such condoms can prevent HIV transmission up to 98 percent of the time.

Condoms should always be used, regardless of whether you know that someone has HIV/AIDS. There are many people with HIV who are sexually active who don't know that they have it. They could have sex with a lot of people before getting any AIDS-related symptoms. This means that all the people they've had sexual experiences with could have gotten HIV without realizing it, too. Then these people can pass it on to other sexual partners, and so on.

Even if both sexual partners know they already have HIV, protection is still needed. There are a number of different strains of HIV. People with one type of HIV can still be at risk of catching another one, too. If they end up becoming infected with more than one strain of HIV, their medical treatment can be more complicated and difficult.

## How do babies get HIV?

If a pregnant woman has HIV, she can pass the virus to her baby. Infection usually happens just before or during delivery, when the baby is exposed to the mother's blood. Without drug intervention during pregnancy, about 20 to 30 percent of newborns of infected mothers may get HIV. With appropriate drug therapy, this can be reduced to just 1 to 2 percent.

Breast milk is another body fluid that can contain HIV. Up to 14 percent of babies of HIV-positive mothers may get HIV from infected breast milk. This is why it is best for mothers with HIV to feed their babies formula instead of breast-feeding them.

# False Fears

## Ways the Virus Is Not Spread

When we first visited Jay after his AIDS diagnosis, we felt uneasy being around him. Because the doctors had confirmed that Jay had HIV/AIDS and not a disease that is transmitted through the air like tuberculosis, we no longer had to wear protective masks and gloves in his room. However, the word *AIDS* caused terrible ideas in my mind, and even though the doctors told us it was safe to be in the room with Jay, I felt more afraid than ever that I could somehow catch the virus from him.

Luckily, I remembered a speech given by Diana, the Princess of Wales, in April of 1991. In it she had said, "HIV does not make people dangerous to know, so you can shake their hands and give them a hug: Heaven knows they need it." I had seen photos and news clips of her, too, shaking hands with AIDS patients. Thanks to her, I found I knew just enough about HIV/AIDS to give Jay a hug on that first visit after his diagnosis.

But when Jay finally came home from the hospital, I was still very aware at all times of the fact that he had AIDS. My mind played tricks on me. When he coughed, I instinctively held my breath, even though I knew I didn't have to do so, because HIV is not passed to others through the air.

I noticed that others in the family were afraid, too. For instance, Jay's mother put paper towels in the bathroom for him to use so he wouldn't have to share regular terry-cloth towels. She served meals using paper plates, cups, and napkins, which could all be thrown away after being used once. None of these measures were necessary because HIV is not spread via towels or eating utensils.

The next summer, at a family picnic with Jay, I heard the distinct whine of a few mosquitoes heading my way. *Mosquitoes — uh-oh — blood!* I thought in a panic, even though I had read that HIV is not transmitted by insects.

It was obvious that we all needed practical information about ordinary real-life situations involving someone with HIV/AIDS.

. . . . . . . . . . . . . . . . . . . . . . . . . . . . . . . . . . . . . . . . . . . . . . . . . . . . . . .

## How long can HIV live outside the body?

Although it is not known *exactly* how long HIV can live outside the body, we do know two important things about its ability to sustain itself. One, HIV is a fragile virus. It is not highly contagious because it dies very quickly once it is outside someone's body. Two, it can't reproduce itself unless it is in the body.

In order to study HIV, scientists have experimented on it under controlled laboratory conditions. They were able to create incredibly high concentrations of the virus that do not exist outside the lab. Under such artificial conditions, HIV can be kept alive for days or weeks. But it is important to remember that these concentrations and conditions are not found anywhere in nature.

Scientists further discovered that when they dried out even these abnormally elevated lab samples, the amount of HIV present dropped by 90 to 99 percent within just several hours. Since the levels of HIV naturally found in HIV-infected human blood or body fluids is so tiny compared with those present in their artificial experiments, scientists concluded that the risk of getting HIV from everyday objects in the environment is essentially zero.

This is how scientists were able to understand why HIV is not highly contagious. It cannot be spread under ordinary circumstances in day-to-day settings, as long as blood, breast milk, or sexual secretions are not present.

## Can you get HIV from saliva?

No. HIV is not transmitted by saliva. A protein in human saliva attaches itself to white blood cells to protect them. It is able to block HIV from infecting them. This is why kissing someone with HIV/AIDS is safe, as long as no blood is present.

## Can you get HIV from tears or sweat?

No. While HIV can be found in tears, the amount is so incredibly small that it does not pose a risk for transmission.

HIV is not present in sweat.

Contact with tears or sweat has never been shown to result in HIV infection when blood is not present.

## Can you get HIV from snot or ear wax?

No. Neither snot nor ear wax is considered a means of HIV infection if no blood is present.

## Can you get HIV from urine or feces?

No. The CDC does not consider excrement (urine or feces) to be a means of HIV infection unless it contains visible blood.

## If someone gets HIV/AIDS, will others in his or her family get it, too?

No. No one gets HIV/AIDS from close daily contact with people who are infected, and HIV/AIDS is not genetic. In general, the entire family will be safe as long as they are careful in any situations that involve blood.

There are certain special situations that might affect families: If a mother had HIV/AIDS while she was pregnant, it would be possible for her to pass it to her baby just before or during childbirth. However, there are now drugs available that can usually prevent this from happening. HIV can also be present in breast milk, so a child should be fed formula instead if the mother is HIV-positive.

Also, since HIV/AIDS can be spread via sex, married couples (like any couples) must use precautions if one or both of them has HIV so that they do not transmit the virus to one another.

## Can insects, like mosquitoes, pass HIV on to people?

No. While some diseases like malaria and yellow fever are transmitted by insect saliva, HIV isn't.

When bloodsucking insects like mosquitoes land somewhere on a human, they inject their own saliva to assist in feeding. They do not inject their own blood or even the blood of the person they bit previously. So you won't get HIV if a mosquito or other insect bites you on a camping or hiking trip or at a picnic or outdoor concert.

## Can you get HIV from things like drinking fountains, phones, toilet seats, or doorknobs?

No. HIV does not live on any of these things. But if any blood is present, be careful not to touch it. Immediately alert an adult to have it cleaned up.

## Can you get HIV/AIDS by being in the same room with someone who has it?

No. HIV is not transmitted though the air. So it is safe to be in a room of any size with someone with HIV/AIDS. This is true even for a really small space like an elevator.

## Is it safe to sit next to someone with HIV at school, home, work, or church?

Yes. HIV is not spread through daily contact with HIV-positive people in any of these situations.

## Can you get HIV from a swimming pool or hot tub?

No. You can't catch HIV by swimming. Even if any HIV-infected cells were present, they would be diluted and destroyed under these circumstances.

## Is it dangerous to share locker rooms, showers, bathrooms, or sports facilities with people who have HIV?

No. These are not places where under ordinary circumstances HIV is spread. You don't get HIV in the same way you would catch a cold or the flu.

## Is it safe to play sports with someone who is HIV-positive?

Yes. Participating in most sports carries almost no risk of getting HIV. This is because these activities don't include contact that involves bleeding. And even if bleeding did occur, HIV could be spread only if infected blood splashed into an uninfected person's mucous membranes (eyes or inside of the nose) or an open cut in their skin. However, in some parts of the United States, HIV-positive athletes are barred from the sport of boxing.

If someone is injured while playing sports, medical experts recommend that trainers and coaches use the same Standard Precautions that health-care workers use when handling blood. This means that they must use latex or plastic gloves when treating wounds. A bleach solution should be used to disinfect any objects that might be splashed with blood. These procedures should be followed in all cases, whether or not any athletes are known to have HIV.

## Could you catch HIV from eating lunch with someone who has the virus?

No. The virus is not transmitted on food that has been touched, shared, or prepared by someone who has it. So you can eat at home, in a restaurant, or anywhere else with someone who is HIV-positive.

## Would you get HIV if you drink from a glass, bottle, or can that someone with HIV has used?

No. You can't catch the virus from objects someone with HIV has handled that are free of blood.

## Shouldn't people with HIV always use plastic forks, knives, and spoons as well as paper cups, plates, napkins, and towels?

No. Using such disposable things is not necessary. The virus is not spread via eating utensils, drinking glasses, or other everyday objects that HIV-infected people have used that are free of blood.

## If you wore the T-shirt or jacket of someone with HIV, would you catch it?

No. The virus is not spread via an infected person's clothes. But do not handle any clothes that have blood on them. Bloody clothes should always be washed with a bleach solution.

## If you babysit for a child with HIV/AIDS, could you catch it from a diaper?

No. People have bathed and diapered babies with HIV or even slept in the same bed with them and not become infected.

The CDC does not consider body wastes to be a means of HIV infection unless they contain visible blood.

## Can pets that live with people who have HIV/AIDS pass it on to people?

No. Most animals can't get or transmit the virus. That's why it's called the *human* immunodeficiency virus. However, some primates, like apes and monkeys, which are closely related to humans, may be able to get or transmit HIV or other viruses in some rare situations. If you are caring for a pet monkey, chimpanzee, or other ape, you should always use Standard Precautions.

Cats do get a disease that is similar to AIDS in people. It is caused by FIV, or feline immunodeficiency virus. The word *feline* refers to an animal of the cat family. However, this virus can't be transmitted to people.

HIV can't be passed from people to cats or any other household pets, either. So it is safe for you to take care of a cat, dog, or bird for someone who has HIV/AIDS.

# Trapped by Stigma

Keeping Jay's Secret

My husband's mother was adamant that no one be told that Jay had HIV/AIDS. *No one* meant no other family members, friends, neighbors, or work colleagues. Jay did not want us to tell anyone either, at first.

Until Jay was diagnosed with HIV/AIDS, I didn't realize that it was still something that people would keep to themselves. I thought that people with HIV/AIDS were more apt to keep it a secret in countries in Africa or in places such as India, China, and Russia. But many people with this virus continue to hide it in the United

States, too. While working on this book, I kept coming up against the secrecy about this disease over and over again.

Because of my mother-in-law's wishes, for a time, my husband and I tried to keep Jay's condition a secret. But the people in our lives could sense that something was terribly wrong.

Finally, we made appointments with our doctor. He helped us to handle the stress and complex emotions that can surface when a family member has HIV/AIDS. Over my mother-in-law's strongest objections, we decided to tell my family, a few of our coworkers, and some of our closest friends because we needed their support. It was a huge relief to be able to share our honest feelings with people who cared about us.

. . . . . . . . . . . . . . . . . . . . . . . . . . . . . . . . . . . . . . . . . . . . . . . . . .

## Why do people with HIV/AIDS sometimes still keep it a secret?

People with HIV/AIDS are often afraid. They are afraid both of having the virus itself and of you finding out that they have it. They are not sure how you will react if they tell you that they are infected. Can they trust you to be kind and understanding, or will you be afraid of them, avoid them, or perhaps even treat them badly?

When people find out that someone has HIV/AIDS, they don't always react in the same way that they might if they learned that the person had another serious illness, like cancer. Instead, they often react with fear and avoidance or by making moral judgments about someone with HIV/AIDS. Because of this, a person with HIV/AIDS who tells people about it might lose his or her friends, job, or home, or even his or her family.

While infected people are battling the virus, they want to keep their lives as normal as possible. To do this, they need their family and friends around them for support. Rather than risk losing them, they sometimes keep quiet.

## Why are some people afraid of people with HIV/AIDS?

Most people are aware that HIV is the virus that causes AIDS. They know that it is infectious and incurable. But many still fear that it is highly contagious. These people mistakenly think that you can get HIV the way you get a cold or the flu—

just by being near someone who has one of these viruses.

There would be a lot less fear if people could understand, once and for all, that HIV/AIDS is not caught and spread in the same way as cold and flu viruses. In some sense, it's like the difference between a cold and an infected finger. If someone has a cold, it is highly contagious. But if someone has an infected finger, you wouldn't catch their infection by just sitting near them. Similarly, HIV cannot be caught through casual contact. It is transmitted only through blood, sexual secretions, or from mother to child during pregnancy or breast-feeding.

## Why do some people seem to dislike or judge those with HIV/AIDS?

When AIDS was first discovered in the United States, it was primarily diagnosed in the gay community, specifically among men who have sex with men. At that time, many people discriminated against those who were gay, and part of the stigma of AIDS was that it was seen as a disease that *only* affected gay people. Now, even though

HIV/AIDS has been widely diagnosed in people of all sexual orientations, some still mistakenly think of it as a "gay disease." Unfortunately, discrimination against gay people has not completely disappeared, and neither has the stigma of AIDS.

Since HIV/AIDS can be spread through illegal drug use or unprotected sex, people may make assumptions or judgments about the behavior of someone with HIV/AIDS. You may even hear people say that those with HIV/AIDS "deserve" to be sick. Often, people who feel this way are being judgmental because they want to tell themselves that they will not catch HIV/AIDS. If they can convince themselves that only people who live a certain way get the disease, then they can feel reassured that they will not catch it themselves. However, HIV/AIDS does not discriminate. It can be spread to anyone through a single encounter with blood, breast milk, or sexual fluids.

No matter how someone gets HIV—whether through sexual intercourse, sharing needles, blood transfusions, or otherwise—no one deserves to get a serious illness. There is nothing shameful about being sick; those with HIV/AIDS deserve our compassion and understanding.

## With all the talk about HIV/AIDS on TV and in the media, does this mean that it's no longer something secret?

No. At present, people are willing to hear about HIV/AIDS on TV and in other forms of media. However, if many of these same people find out that someone in their own neighborhood, school, or circle of family and friends has HIV/AIDS, they may react with fear, anger, or discrimination. It is one thing to know about the virus that causes AIDS, and it is quite another thing to know a person who has it. Talking openly about AIDS on TV is a good first step, but until people can feel comfortable with HIV-positive people in their daily lives, we still have a long way to go.

## Does everyone with HIV/AIDS keep it a secret?

No, many people do speak out about their HIV status.

Rock Hudson, the movie star, told the media that he had AIDS in 1985, just before he died.

Magic Johnson, the basketball star, revealed that

he was HIV-positive in 1991. He has been an AIDS activist ever since.

Arthur Ashe, the tennis star, announced that he had AIDS in 1992. He died in 1993.

Greg Louganis, the Olympic diver, announced in 1995 that he had contracted HIV. He, too, has become a spokesperson regarding this pandemic.

Private citizens have formed HIV-positive support groups and many other helpful groups that one by one are transforming the perception of HIV/AIDS in their communities. They have become a force for good.

## What are some of the advantages to being open about HIV/AIDS?

There are many good reasons for people to be open about their HIV-positive status. On a personal level, it allows them to receive the emotional support that they need, taking a huge burden off patients and their families. Those who are able to be open about their status may be surprised by the positive reaction and support that they receive from those around them. In addition, each person who speaks candidly about his or her experiences with HIV/AIDS shows the people around them that HIV/AIDS is not a mysterious disease that affects only people they don't know, but a disease that matters to all of us. Speaking openly about HIV/AIDS can also help to prevent the spread of the disease, as it makes everyone more aware of the ways HIV/AIDS is and is not transmitted. Finally, by speaking to their friends and family or to a wider audience about their disease, people with HIV/AIDS may inspire others to do the same.

## Why do some parents object to their children being taught about HIV/AIDS in school?

One of the main ways that people get HIV/AIDS is through sex. So in order to talk about HIV/AIDS, you have to talk about sex, too.

Some parents believe that this kind of teaching should only happen at home. But since HIV/AIDS is a public health issue, schools can play a vital role in prevention.

It is important that young people begin to learn about HIV/AIDS *before* they begin to think a lot about sex. Without the right health and safety information, people can't make informed choices about sexual behavior. This increases their risk of getting HIV or other serious sexually transmitted diseases.

## What can you do if someone at school says cruel things about a friend or family member with HIV/AIDS?

The best option would be to tell an adult you trust—a teacher, counselor, school nurse, administrator, or family member—about it, so that he or she can help you to put a stop to the situation. But if there isn't anyone at school or at home you can safely confide in, perhaps you can try contacting one of the AIDS service organizations listed at the end of this book for help. Such groups often provide confidential education and support to both people with HIV and those who know and care about them.

If people are spreading misinformation and you feel comfortable correcting them, you can try to explain the things you've learned about HIV/AIDS. Perhaps you could even show them this book.

## What can you do if people don't want to visit you because a family member has HIV/AIDS?

Even with all the information about how it is safe to be around someone with HIV/AIDS in everyday situations, some people are very afraid of it. They may still believe that you can get HIV/AIDS from casual contact, even though this is not the case. You may not be able to convince your friends to visit you, but you can try to teach them that it's not dangerous to be around your family member. They might have some questions that are answered in this book.

## What should you do if your parents want you to keep it a secret that a family member has HIV/AIDS?

If your family feels this strongly about it, you should try to respect their wishes. But if you want to talk about it, you could ask your doctor or an AIDS service organization if there is a confidential support group for kids who have family members with HIV/AIDS.

You could also write your thoughts in a journal or diary. These are great places to express your feelings about things.

Although you may feel isolated right now, you are not alone. Lots of people all over the world are in your situation.

## Are there laws that protect people with HIV/AIDS from discrimination?

Yes. Courts, legislatures, and other institutions in the United States have attempted to protect people with HIV/AIDS from discrimination. For instance, people with HIV/AIDS are covered under the Americans with Disabilities Act of 1990, which prohibits discrimination in the workplace and ensures equal access to public places, transportation, and government services.

# Hit by a Ton of Bricks

## The Emotional Toll

It's hard to describe how intense our feelings were when we first learned that Jay had AIDS. Have you ever heard the expression to feel as if you were "hit by a ton of bricks"? That's how it felt. A huge weight had landed on us.

We were just trying to adjust to the fact that Jay was HIV-positive, when a few days later we were told he had AIDS and less than six months to live. At that time in the epidemic, AIDS was a death sentence.

I was so upset that my arms, legs, and body felt constricted, as if I had tight bands wrapped around me. It was a strange sensation.

I couldn't sleep at night.

During the day, I couldn't concentrate on anything. Usually, I like to read. However, I found I couldn't keep my mind focused long enough to read more than a few sentences at a time. Neither my husband nor I could watch much television, either. Because of our emotional state, everything on television seemed maddening and meaningless.

We were just too sad to do much of anything for a while. One of the reasons I'm writing this book is to say that HIV/AIDS affects the whole family psychologically, not just the person who is sick. It takes an enormous emotional toll.

The ongoing stress of having a member of the family with HIV/AIDS causes emotional meltdowns. People's tempers flare up. There can be a lot of anger and mixed feelings for all concerned.

. . . . . . . . . . . . . . . . . . . . . . . . . . . . . . . . . . . . . . . . . . . . . . . . . .

# What are some common ways that people react when they're told they have HIV/AIDS?

Learning the results of an HIV test is very difficult when it shows people that they are infected with this virus. People can react to a positive test with sadness, fear, and anger.

Although HIV/AIDS can be treated as a chronic disease, there is still no cure. Living with HIV/AIDS, while knowing they can die from it, is very scary for those who have the disease. Not knowing when, where, or how they might die adds to the fear. They probably also worry about how the people they know will handle it if and when they do die. All of this puts them under a terrible strain. They may experience anger and mood swings as they try to face an uncertain future.

Another common emotion people experience when they are told they have an incurable medical condition like HIV/AIDS is denial. Denial is a refusal to believe that something is true. This is a natural first reaction, especially because someone with HIV may still feel completely healthy. It allows time for the person to adjust to the new situation.

Some people who are diagnosed with HIV/AIDS may want to talk about it; some may not. If your friend or family member has HIV/AIDS, let him or her know that you're there to listen if he or she needs you.

## How long will you feel overwhelmed by the news that someone in your family has HIV/AIDS?

Since there is no cure yet for HIV/AIDS, you are reacting in a perfectly normal way. At first, it may be very hard to deal with your family member's condition, and you may feel sad, fearful, or angry.

There's no specific timetable for these emotions, but after a while, the shock does begin to wear off. In time, you will be able to adjust to the situation. It is very important that you take care of yourself, too. Do get help from a health professional, counselor, or trusted adult if you continue to feel overwhelmed.

## After finding out that someone in your family has HIV/AIDS, why might you have trouble sleeping, concentrating, or being around your friends?

If someone close to you has HIV/AIDS, you may feel that you are removed from ordinary life for a while. You are seeing things from a different perspective. Not being able to focus on things is one way our minds react to a highly stressful situation. Eventually, though, your mind will adapt, and you'll be able to go about your day-to-day activities more easily.

Sleeplessness is also common after a life-changing event. It may pass after a few days, but if you continue to be unable to sleep, this may be due to the deep sadness or even depression you are feeling. In this case, tell your family right away. They can get you help from a counselor or doctor for your sleep problem.

If you're worried about your concentration or if your grades become a concern, you may want to talk with a counselor and/or teacher at school to let them know that there is a family medical crisis at home. They may have some suggestions for you on how to handle your schoolwork as you adjust to your family's situation.

It's OK to need time by yourself at first to try to adapt to the new circumstances in your family. You may also think you can't show your true feelings to people, especially your own family, if you're trying to be strong for them. But whenever things seem too difficult to bear, seek help from a counselor or trusted friend. You don't have to face this alone.

Remember, there are support groups in most communities for kids who have family members with HIV/AIDS. They offer a safe and confidential place where you can be open with your feelings.

## How might your parents' behavior toward you change if someone in your family has HIV/AIDS?

Your mom and dad will probably feel overwhelmed by your family member's serious medical condition. They could be so overwhelmed that they can't even talk about it.

They will probably also be very busy and tired. If your family member is very sick, there may be a lot of things they must do to take care of him, such as giving him medicines, bathing him, and driving him to the doctor. Others in the family often feel the strain when a relative is seriously ill.

You might feel as if your parents don't have time for you now. Remember that they are grateful that you are well. They probably think that you are OK and they don't need to worry about you. They most likely feel that you must already know that you are, and always will be, an important part of your family.

Your parents will probably feel very sad about your family member's condition. You may even hear them say that they don't want to live anymore. This doesn't mean that they don't think you are just as important as your family member who is sick. It's just a way of expressing their immense sadness.

Suppose you had two pets. If one of them were really sick, you would feel quite sad. This doesn't mean that you don't love or care about the pet that is healthy. But even though the pet that is well can't protect you from being sad, it can give you some comfort. In the same way, just by being you, you give your parents comfort.

It would be great if you could talk about your feelings with everyone involved. But if this is not possible, you can always write down your thoughts in a journal or diary. You can do some artwork to express yourself, too.

## Why don't people ever ask how you feel, too, or even take just a little interest in you now?

If your family member is seriously ill, sometimes people may forget that there are other important people, like you, in the household. They know they can't make your family member well, but they try to lift his or her spirits by bringing gifts or paying lots of attention to him or her.

Fortunately, you are not sick, but your life has been greatly changed by your family member's illness. The people you know may not realize that you could use some attention and encouragement, too. If you can, try to talk to them about your feelings.

# Slowly Stealing Life

Jay's Treatment and Side Effects

After Jay's pneumonia improved, he was released from the hospital. However, he was too ill to return to his job or even to live on his own. He had to move in with his parents.

The hospital referred Jay to a doctor who was a specialist in AIDS medicine. Many doctors now devote their entire practices to helping HIV/AIDS patients. Jay had to continue taking strong antibiotics to keep his lungs clear. The doctor gave him other medicines to try to manage his symptoms, including the emotional ones such as depression.

Jay felt that AIDS was slowly stealing his life. He spent most of his time resting, taking pills, and going to the doctor.

Later that fall, Jay's AIDS doctor learned of a new treatment that showed some promise. This was the so-called AIDS cocktail, a combination of drugs that was given to try to slow or stop the virus from replicating, or copying, itself, reducing the amount of virus present in his body.

Jay had to swallow dozens of red, blue, yellow, orange, purple, and white pills each day at very specific times. Some had to be taken with meals and some without food.

It was a very strict regimen. The doctor told him that it could be dangerous for him to forget to take any of the medicines. If he did, the drugs might stop working, the viral levels in his body would rise, and he could die. Also, if many AIDS patients stopped following their proper treatment, this could contribute to the development of drug-resistant strains of HIV.

Jay's experience was not unusual at the time he was diagnosed, but today, things have improved greatly. Many HIV/AIDS patients now only need to take one or two pills a day. This regime is much easier to follow, and provides a huge improvement to patients' quality of life.

## Drug-Resistant Strains of HIV

It is the nature of viruses that they change as they replicate, or copy, themselves. The HIV that escapes being blocked by the drugs that stop it from copying itself continues to live on. It replicates again and again. It is no longer affected by the drugs and is said to be drug resistant.

At Christmastime that year, I really did not know what to get for Jay as a gift. The doctors said he had only a few more months to live. I finally decided to give him a book on saints that I knew had interested him before he was sick.

With treatment, gradually over time, Jay got stronger. He gained weight. He could walk unassisted to a nearby beach.

By the following Christmas, I was able to give him two presents: a watch and a calendar. He had more time. It was a miracle.

The miracle eventually enabled him to live on his own again. Jay was lucky that his employer was understanding about his illness, and happily, he was able to return to work a year or so later.

However, the AIDS medicines Jay took were very toxic. The pills at that time were strong, and many of them had potentially serious life-threatening side effects of their own. Some were known to cause kidney and liver failure, heart attacks, and other very serious or fatal illnesses. So as time went by, Jay paid a steep price for his miracle. The same drugs that were destroying the virus in his body were causing other grave health problems.

Fortunately, the new drugs now used to treat HIV/AIDS are much less toxic and easier for people to take. This is another part of the success story in fighting this disease.

· · · · · · · · · · · · · · · · · · · · · · · · · · · · · · · · · · · · · · · · · · · · · · · · · · · ·

## What are the symptoms of HIV/AIDS?

Many people with HIV don't even realize that they have it.

Two to eight weeks after people are infected, they might have a brief flu-like illness with a high fever and a sore throat. It could be accompanied by swollen lymph nodes. Some may have a rash, diarrhea, vomiting, or thrush (a yeast infection in the mouth). These conditions usually last from one to four weeks but can last up to a few months. Usually these symptoms clear up by themselves, and people with HIV could feel well for many years.

Over time, if left untreated as the number of T cells in their blood declines, people with HIV begin to develop a range of AIDS-related symptoms such as fevers, night sweats, unexplained weight loss and/or fatigue, severe diarrhea, stomach and general pain, and swollen lymph nodes that do not go away on their own. People with AIDS may have other persistent symptoms such as unexplained coughs, sore throats, yeast infections, and purplish lesions on the skin.

Having AIDS means that a person's immune system is very weak or exhausted and cannot fight infections effectively. Without treatment at this point, in addition to infections of the lungs, the brain and eyes may be affected. Some people with AIDS may lose their ability to think clearly. Some become blind. Since their immune systems are broken down, their bodies may also not be able fight off other serious diseases such as cancer. To say what all the symptoms for each of these might be would take a separate book in itself.

## What is the treatment for HIV/AIDS?

HIV/AIDS is managed as a chronic illness whenever possible. This means that a person with HIV who is diagnosed soon after infection and takes his or her medicines may be able to live out a normal life span. Antiviral drugs control the level of HIV in the body by interfering with its ability to replicate, or copy, itself.

During treatment, the amount of the virus present in the body drops, so the person usually feels healthy for a long time.

HIV/AIDS is a complex disease that may affect every person differently, so doctors usually treat each person individually rather than using one way for everyone.

There is lots of ongoing research about HIV/AIDS, so new and exciting strategies for treatment of HIV/AIDS are appearing all the time. For instance, early in 2008, scientists reported the discovery of 273 human proteins that, if blocked, could keep the HIV virus in check. Of these, only 36 were previously known to interact with HIV. This gives researchers more than 200 new targets for anti-HIV drugs. It is another major breakthrough.

## Why do doctors need to count T cells called CD4 cells to treat HIV/AIDS?

When someone is infected with HIV for a long time, the number of CD4 cells they have (their CD4 cell count) goes down. This is a sign that their immune system is being weakened. The lower the CD4 cell count, the more likely it is that the person will get sick. Monitoring a person's CD4 cell count is an important part of medical treatment for HIV/AIDS.

A healthy person usually has a CD4 count of between 500 to 1,600. If someone with HIV has a CD4 count of 500 or more, this is considered good. However, if the count drops to 200 or less, a person with HIV now is said to have AIDS.

## What does "viral load" mean?

"Viral load" means the amount of HIV present in an infected person's blood. Viral loads are usually reported as the number of copies of HIV in one milliliter of blood. The viral load tests count up to about one million copies and are always being improved so as to be more sensitive.

## Why do doctors test for viral load when they are treating HIV/AIDS patients?

Doctors test for viral load to see if a particular treatment is helping to reduce the amount of HIV present in a patient's body.

The lower the viral load, the better, and this seems to mean a longer, healthier life.

## What does it mean if a person with HIV has a viral load that is "undetectable"?

This is the best possible test result. However, it does not mean that there is no virus present in the blood. It just means that there is not enough to find and count. There is no "safe" level of viral load. If an infected person's viral load is undetectable, they are less likely to pass HIV to another person, but it is still possible. Standard Precautions should always be used.

## What are some side effects of HIV/AIDS drugs?

Compared to the drugs used early in the AIDS epidemic, the modern medications have very few side effects. Some people experience nausea, dizziness, headaches, diarrhea, or insomnia. Despite these effects, people need to stay on the antiviral drugs because these medicines reduce the amount of HIV in the body.

## What are the long-term effects of taking HIV/AIDS medicines?

The long-term effects of the HIV/AIDS drugs are not yet known. However, these medicines are much less toxic than those that were used at earlier times in the epidemic. So doctors are very hopeful that people can stay on these antiviral drugs for many years without serious problems.

## If HIV/AIDS is now treatable as a chronic disease, then it's not such a big deal to get it anymore, is it?

This completely misses the point. Diabetes is a chronic disease. Multiple sclerosis (MS) is a chronic disease. Tuberculosis (TB) is a chronic disease. Some cancers can be treated like a chronic disease.

That doesn't mean that these diseases aren't a big deal. They can have an enormous impact on people's health and quality of life. If people knew how to avoid coming down with any of these illnesses, they certainly would do so.

There are lots of diseases we don't yet know how to prevent. The good news for everyone is that HIV/AIDS is almost always preventable.

# Lifelines
## Still Be a Friend

Jay finally decided to reach out to just one friend to say that he had AIDS. Even though the person did not reject Jay, the experience was not helpful. It made Jay hesitant to approach anyone else for a long time.

Jay's friend told him that everything he was doing to fight the virus was wrong, that the drugs he was taking were poisonous, that the foods he was eating should be different, and so on. Jay's friend meant well, but what Jay really needed at that moment was to have a friend just listen and care. Anyone with HIV/AIDS needs this kind of lifeline. Fortunately for Jay, later on he did tell a few other friends that he was sick. Along with his family, these friends became lifelines for him throughout his illness.

While I was working on this book, a friend of mine told me that her mother had died of AIDS two years previously.

Apparently, Nan, her mom, had to have an emergency blood transfusion during what was an otherwise fairly routine operation. Later on, the family found out that the blood was tainted. At that time, the blood supply was not tested as it is now for the presence of HIV. Nan became quite sick. It was years before the doctors finally diagnosed her condition as AIDS.

Nan was very active in her community, so while she was ill, she had lots of visitors. However, once her friends found out that she had AIDS, there was always one reason or another why they couldn't visit her anymore. She spent the last months of her life with just her immediate family around her.

If you find out that someone you know has HIV/AIDS, the first and most important thing of all is to still be a friend.

. . . . . . . . . . . . . . . . . . . . . . . . . . . . . . . . . . . . . . . . . . . . . . . . . .

## How can you be a good friend to someone with HIV/AIDS?

If someone has HIV/AIDS, it doesn't make him or her dangerous to know. You can continue to do the things that you'd normally do when you hang out together. You should treat your friend like all of your other friends — and that includes using Standard Precautions in situations involving blood or other body fluids.

Your friend may want to talk to you about his or her fears about having HIV. Be a good listener, just as you would if your friend wanted to share any other problem.

Even if you have a friend with AIDS who is seriously ill, your friend is still not dangerous to know. You can touch his or her hand or give him or her a hug. If your friend is too weak to see you, you can still call him or her. You could also send a text message, e-mail, card, or note. Your friend will appreciate knowing that you are thinking about him or her.

People with HIV/AIDS, like all of us, want to live and enjoy life as long as they possibly can. Part of doing this is having a friend, like you, to joke around with and confide in.

## Can you still be friends with people who have HIV/AIDS even if your family doesn't think it's a good idea?

Just because someone has HIV/AIDS, it does not make him or her less of a friend. It is still safe to be around the person in everyday situations. And, if anything, he or she needs friends and fun now more than ever.

If your parents have health concerns about you visiting a friend with HIV/AIDS, you could show them this book or have them talk to your doctor. If they still won't allow you to go to your friend's house, you can find ways to stay in touch. For instance, take the time to text-message, e-mail, or phone your friend.

## If a friend tells you that she or someone she cares about has HIV/AIDS, what should you say?

Just say whatever you would say if she told you the person had cancer or any other serious illness.

First, express concern and compassion. She'll probably want to share her feelings with you about it. So if you're able to be a good listener, this is all that is really needed at this point.

But please try not to let the question "How did he get it?" be the first sentence that comes out of your mouth. I had a friend say this to me when I first told her that Jay had AIDS. I felt angry. I would have welcomed a kind word instead. It may be a natural question, but it sounds as if the asker is placing the blame on the person who is ill.

I answered her question by saying, "He got it from a virus." Then I quickly ended the conversation.

I don't think people who ask this question mean to be insensitive. It's quite simple. They remain afraid of HIV/AIDS since there is no cure yet, so they are always trying to reassure themselves that they won't catch it, too.

## If you visit someone in the hospital who has AIDS, will you get the virus?

No. You won't get this virus this way. You can't get HIV/AIDS from the air or by touching or hugging someone who has it. HIV/AIDS is not transmitted either through the air or through casual contact.

However, if you have a cold or the flu, it's not a good idea to visit your friend. Colds and the flu are highly contagious. People with AIDS can't fight off infections the way a person with a healthy immune system can, so it's especially important that they not be exposed unnecessarily to germs. If you are sick yourself, it is best to speak by phone rather than visit in person.

# Many Small Deaths

## Jay's Final Days

Jay, like many others who had AIDS in the mid-1990s, eventually became very ill. He was forced to give up, one by one, many things that were once very important to him. Having to do this is a kind of death. It's the death of a way of life.

Unfortunately, even though Jay loved his job, he eventually had to stop working permanently. Once a highly energetic person and the life of the party, Jay became withdrawn and tired all the time. He slept ten hours or more at night. During the day he often took naps that lasted for five hours. Sometimes he slept all day.

There were many times when Jay was so sick that we thought he could be dying. We went through this situation over and over again. It was hard on him, and it was hard on us, too. Each time it happened, I started to feel those bands of fear and sadness tightening around me again.

Jay hated it when people tried to make him feel better by saying that anybody could die tomorrow. They would tell him that a car could hit anyone at any time and it could be fatal. Jay said that having AIDS is like watching a car come toward you in slow motion. You know it's going to hit you. You know it's going to kill you. But there is nothing you can do.

Over time the doctor had to keep changing Jay's drug regimen as his current one became ineffective against HIV. Each time we wondered if he would be able to tolerate the side effects of the new medicines.

These days, the medications don't wear out as often as they used to in the past. Doctors now anticipate and have evidence that a single drug regimen will keep HIV in check for decades. But when Jay was sick, this wasn't the case.

During the spring and summer of 2006, there was more bad news. Jay was diagnosed with an opportunistic infection, a deadly form of skin cancer for which he underwent two surgeries. He grew even more thin and weak. He withdrew from nearly everyone but his little dog.

My husband talked with Jay about hospice and other types of medical support. He began the search for end-of-life care for his brother.

Unfortunately, very soon after this conversation, Jay died at home during the first week of September in the early evening.

A few days before he died, Jay told me that his mother wanted him to go to the doctor because he was in such a weakened state. Throughout the eleven years he was ill, Jay had hardly ever spoken about his pain and suffering. However, this time he said, "Mom doesn't understand that I'm so sick of doctors and hospitals."

When Jay died, we felt numb. His death had been hanging over us for such a long time that when he was finally gone, it felt unreal. Once again, we all had trouble sleeping. We became more and more tired.

We also had some unpleasant surprises. Jay's landlord told us that she would never have rented the property to Jay had she known he had AIDS. More than twenty-five years into the HIV/AIDS crisis, we learned firsthand that some people still discriminate against those with this disease.

Even in death, AIDS can hide. Jay's mother told everyone that he died of skin cancer. In Jay's obituary, or notice of his death, AIDS was not mentioned. This is not unusual. Often AIDS may not be listed as the cause of death in an obituary. Instead, families may write cancer, heart disease, or merely, "after a long illness."

So, even in death, the secrecy can remain.

. . . . . . . . . . . . . . . . . . . . . . . . . . . . . . . . . . . . . . . . . . . . . .

## Do people with AIDS still die?

Yes, some people with AIDS do still die, especially if they are not receiving treatment. However, there are not as many deaths as there were earlier in the epidemic, and those who begin treatment early for their HIV infection have a good chance of having a long and relatively healthy life.

## If someone has HIV/AIDS, how long can he or she live?

There is no way to give an exact answer to this question. Each individual situation is different. However, with treatment, HIV can be considered a chronic disease such as diabetes or MS. This is why it is vital for people, particularly those who are sexually active, to be routinely tested for HIV. On average, without treatment, it takes about eleven years for a person with HIV to get AIDS. Without medical help at this point, he or she will suffer serious and life-threatening medical problems.

At one point in the pandemic, people with AIDS were considered long-term survivors if they lived five years or more. However, there are new and more effective treatments being developed all the time. People may be able to live a long time with it. So we now say that people are living with AIDS rather than dying of it.

## Why don't the AIDS medicines make people well?

The current AIDS drugs treat but can't cure AIDS.

When people have AIDS, their immune systems are damaged. Some of the medicines they take lower the amount of HIV in their bodies. Other drugs manage the various symptoms they may have as a result of a weakened immune system.

However, while these drugs may keep people's immune systems from further deteriorating, they are not always able to rebuild them. In such cases, the medicines may help people with HIV/AIDS to live longer, but they cannot make them well.

## If someone with AIDS is very sick, will he or she die right away?

Nobody can accurately predict the life span of someone with AIDS — or of anyone else, for that matter. There are too many individual circumstances. There may be lots of ups and downs in the medical condition of people with AIDS. They might have crises when they are intensely ill and near death. Then all of a sudden, within a matter of weeks, they may return to regular life. This may happen again and again.

This is difficult for everyone involved, especially the AIDS patients themselves. When they are feeling somewhat better, in the back of their minds, they always wonder how long it will be before they will be dangerously ill again.

Remember the story about the boy who cried "Wolf!"? He shouted "Wolf!" so many times that when he really saw a wolf, people didn't believe him. The situation with AIDS is sort of like this. Families have sat at the bedside of an AIDS patient when he or she is deathly ill. Yet the person doesn't die. It is impossible to know which medical crisis will be the final one.

Since the person with AIDS is still here, the

family can't grieve as fully as they will when death finally happens. But they can't feel happy, either, because they know that the person with AIDS will probably become sick again.

## What kind of care is available for a family member with AIDS who is too sick to remain at home?

Your family member's doctor can discuss the options available in this situation. Hospice may be one possibility. This is a community-based organization that provides end-of-life care and support to patients and those who love them.

## When a family member dies of AIDS, why do some families not talk about it?

Some people have a hard time speaking at all about death. And because of the secrecy and stigma that can surround AIDS, your family may be even more reluctant to talk about your family member's death.

Even if no one in your immediate family will share their feelings, there are usually community support groups for family members of those who have AIDS. You could reach out for help from one of these groups or from a school counselor or clergy member. These resources will offer confidential support.

## What are some of the symptoms of grief?

Grief is very personal, and it is such a complicated topic that entire books have been written about it. Reactions to a loss such as the death of someone in your life can involve a whole range of emotions. Some symptoms may show up as physical ones such as headaches or stomachaches. Others can be mental reactions such as nightmares or sleep disturbances. Still more are behavioral ones such as becoming withdrawn or aggressive. You may feel emotions such as numbness, sadness, anger, or anxiety. You might also feel lost, empty, guilty, or abandoned. Remember, each person's experience is different. There is no right or wrong way to grieve.

## If a family member dies of AIDS, how long will it take to adjust?

Grief is a natural response to loss. There is no time-table for grieving. People grieve in their own way and heal at their own pace. In a way, it's a lifelong process. For instance, if your family member always attended your birthday parties, you may miss him or her and feel sad on that day every year.

In addition to speaking with trusted friends and adults about this, you can contact community groups such as hospice for help. Such organizations have bereavement support groups for people who are dealing with loss. Many even have special groups for children and teens.

## Why are some people with HIV/AIDS suicidal?

Even though HIV/AIDS is now considered a chronic illness, it is still incurable, so being diagnosed with it can sometimes trigger severe depression and despair. Some people with HIV/AIDS may also feel very isolated, scared, and overwhelmed.

If someone you know is talking about suicide and asking you to keep it a secret, this is not OK.

Suicide is not something anyone should have to keep secret. It is very important for you to seek immediate help from a physician, counselor, clergy member, or trusted adult.

If a friend does commit suicide, it's important to remember that no matter what, his death was not your fault. It is possible that your friend had other issues in addition to HIV/AIDS that contributed to his despair.

## What are some private ways to remember a friend who has died of HIV/AIDS?

You can use your creativity to come up with special ways to remember your friend. For example, you could design an online tribute to the person. Memory books and memory boxes are other ways to preserve memories. A memory book is a scrapbook you create using words, photographs, and art to celebrate someone's life. A memory box holds objects that have meaning associated with the person who died. These objects might be anything such a shell, a lucky penny, or a even a toy that he or she gave you when you were young.

## What are some public ways to remember a friend who has died of HIV/AIDS?

Nothing can bring back your friend, but one way of handling the difficult things you experience in life is to find ways of transforming them into something positive. As a way of honoring your friend who died, you might want to consider wearing an AIDS ribbon, going on an AIDS walk, attending an AIDS Candlelight Memorial, creating a panel for the AIDS Memorial Quilt, or becoming a peer counselor for HIV/AIDS education.

## What is the AIDS ribbon?

The AIDS ribbon was created by the artist Frank Moore and a group of professionals in the art community called Visual AIDS in 1991. Mr. Moore remembers, "My neighbors in upstate New York had a daughter in the [first] Gulf War, and they tied a yellow ribbon around a tree in their yard. It wasn't a political thing, just a gesture of support for their child. I took that idea and suggested that we turn it into something you could wear." The ribbon is red because AIDS is a blood-borne disease. It is worn by people both with and without HIV/AIDS to symbolize that we are all connected. Everyone is affected by HIV/AIDS in one way or another. It's a global problem we all share.

## What is World AIDS Day?

World AIDS Day is a day set aside each year on December 1 to show support for those who have AIDS and to remember those who have died of this disease. Each year an AIDS-related theme is highlighted. It is a worldwide day of AIDS education and awareness. The first World AIDS Day was held on December 1, 1988. It quickly gained the support of the World Health Organization of the United Nations.

## What is the AIDS Memorial Quilt?

The AIDS Memorial Quilt was developed by Cleve Jones, an activist, in 1985. When he learned that more than 1,000 people in San Francisco had died of AIDS, he encouraged their friends and relatives to write the names of their loved ones on placards. When these were taped together on the walls of a public building, they looked like a quilt.

In 1986, Mr. Jones created the first cloth panel for a quilt in memory of his friend Marvin Feldman, who died of AIDS. By 1987, almost 2,000 panels had been made for the AIDS Memorial Quilt by people from all over the world. During that year, it was displayed for the first time in Washington, D.C. It covered an area larger than a football field. The quilt has been shown, in whole or in part, thousands of times.

By 2001, the quilt had more than 46,000 panels and covered more than twenty-five football fields. New panels continue to arrive daily. On December 1, 1996, it was displayed online for the first time as part of the World AIDS Day activities. Due to the enormous size of the quilt, it is now displayed only in sections.

## What is the International AIDS Candlelight Memorial?

The International AIDS Candlelight Memorial is the world's largest annual HIV/AIDS event. It honors the memory of those lost to HIV/AIDS and shows support for those currently living with HIV and AIDS. The International AIDS Candlelight

Memorial also works to decrease the stigma related to HIV/AIDS. In addition, it raises community awareness as it fights against the spread of HIV/AIDS. The first International AIDS Candlelight Memorial was held in 1983, early on in the history of the epidemic. Observances of the memorial differ from community to community. In some places, only a few people gather with candles in hand. In others, thousands march with candles through the streets to commemorate those affected by HIV/AIDS. People are free to organize an AIDS Candlelight Memorial in any way they wish.

# A Vision of Hope

Another Family Story

America has come a long way toward bringing HIV/ AIDS out into the open thanks to efforts by activists, educators, and those brave enough to tell their stories. But we still have a long way to go until all people with HIV/AIDS and their families feel safe enough to tell others they have this virus as they would if they had an illness such as cancer. Until that time, HIV/AIDS will continue to be a disease surrounded by secrecy.

I want to end this book by telling you another family story.

When I was in fifth grade, my mom almost died. Doctors operated on her leg after she was in a terrible skiing accident. Unfortunately, she developed some serious medical complications. Blood clots formed in her leg. These clots were not discovered until they had moved to her lungs. If they were not treated, they could have traveled to her brain and heart, killing her instantly.

My mom's hospital stay lasted for many weeks. She was in great danger until the blood clots dissolved. It was a tough time for our whole family. I was very scared, but lots of people gave me support, and my friends and their parents often asked me how my mom was doing. At school, my classmates and teachers talked to me about her to make sure that I was OK, too. Both my grandmothers took turns staying with my sister and me whenever my father was at work or at the hospital.

Finally, my mom did get better. With all the help and concern, my father, sister, and I were all right, too.

I look forward to a time in the future when if I were in fifth grade and, instead of a serious skiing accident, my mother had HIV/AIDS, the story I just told you would not change very much. Having a family member with HIV/AIDS should not be very different from having one with a broken leg, cancer, or nearly any other medical condition.

I know this is possible because of something a friend of mine who has had cancer told me. Apparently, many years ago, people were very afraid of those with cancer, too. They thought they would catch cancer just by being near them. Now this wouldn't even enter our minds. That's progress.

This will eventually happen with HIV/AIDS, too.

I look forward to a time when no one with HIV/AIDS has to remain anonymous anymore in America or anywhere else in the world.

. . . . . . . . . . . . . . . . . . . . . . . . . . . . . . . . . . . . . . . . . . . . . . . . . . . . . .

# WHERE TO FIND MORE INFORMATION ABOUT HIV/AIDS

This book has been difficult to write and even more so to finish. Each time I thought I had learned enough to complete the project, there would be a new medical crisis for Jay or a wave of new information about HIV/AIDS.

Every effort has been made to make the text of this book as accurate as possible, according to the sources available at the time of writing. I have consulted experts in the field of HIV/AIDS—doctors, counselors, and researchers—to review the information in this book. However, sometimes new research changes medical knowledge and thinking, so be sure to look at the websites listed below for the latest up-to-date information about HIV/AIDS.

**GENERAL INFORMATION ABOUT HIV/AIDS**
**www.aegis.com**
The largest HIV/AIDS knowledge base in the world

**www.aidsinfonet.org**
A project of the New Mexico AIDS Education and Training Center at the University of New Mexico School of Medicine that has become an international resource for information on HIV/AIDS

www.cdc.gov
The United States Centers for Disease Control and Prevention's website; includes information on Standard Precautions

www.grassrootsoccer.org
A nonprofit organization that uses the power of sports to reach children with life-saving information about HIV prevention

www.redcross.org
Go to the sub-menu Health and Safety Services for information about the American Red Cross's HIV/AIDS awareness and prevention programs

www.teenaids.org
A nonprofit organization dedicated to educating young people about HIV/AIDS

www.thebody.com
A good resource for general information about HIV/AIDS

www.unaids.org
The Joint United Nations Programme on HIV/AIDS

www.webMD.com
For general information about treatment and related issues

www.youthaids.org
An education and prevention program that uses media, pop culture, music, theater, and sports to help stop the spread of HIV/AIDS

## HELPING PEOPLE WITH HIV/AIDS

**www.campheartland.org**
A nonprofit organization called One Heartland runs summer camps for HIV-positive kids and their families, as well as AIDS support, education, and prevention programs.

**www.pawssf.org**
PAWS (Pets Are Wonderful Support), a San Francisco–based nonprofit organization devoted to caring for the pets of people with HIV/AIDS

## REMEMBERING PEOPLE WITH HIV/AIDS

**www.aidsquilt.org**
The AIDS Memorial Quilt and the Names Project Foundation

**www.candlelightmemorial.org**
The International AIDS Candlelight Memorial. Light a candle online and find out when and where the memorial is held near you.

**www.nhpco.org**
The National Hospice and Palliative Care Organization. Consult your local hospice organizations for support groups for grieving children and teens.

**www.worldaidsday.org**
World AIDS Day is on December 1. Remember to wear the red ribbon!

## HOTLINES

GENERAL INFORMATION ABOUT HIV/AIDS

CDC National HIV/AIDS Hotlines

1-800-CDC-INFO (232-4636) For questions about HIV/AIDS

1-888-232-6348 For hearing-impaired persons

1-800-458-5231 For the Prevention Information Network

# GLOSSARY

**abstinence:** a decision to avoid sexual activity (oral, anal, or vaginal)

**AIDS:** acquired immune deficiency syndrome, a life-threatening disease of the human immune system in which large numbers of the cells that fight infections are destroyed

**AIDS cocktail:** a mixture of various drugs that work together to suppress HIV

**anal sex:** sex in which a penis is inserted into the anus

**antibiotics:** drugs that are used in medicine to kill or prevent the growth of harmful germs

**antibodies:** substances produced by the body's white blood cells to fight germs that cause disease

**antiviral drugs:** chemical substances used in medicine to stop or slow the growth of a virus

**bone marrow:** soft tissue that fills the cavities of most bones

**CD4 cell:** a "helper" T cell, which attacks infections in the body

**CD8 cell:** a "suppressor" T cell, which ends the immune response; it is also a "killer" T cell, since it destroys cancer cells and cells infected with a virus.

**cells:** the smallest basic units of all living matter in plants and animals; they are made up of protoplasm surrounded by a membrane.

**chronic:** lasting a long time or recurring often

**condom:** a protective barrier made of latex or polyurethane used to prevent pregnancy and/or the transmission of sexually transmitted diseases (STDs)

**contagious:** capable of being spread by casual contact from one person to another

**denial:** a refusal to accept or believe that something is true

**diabetes:** a disease marked by an insulin deficiency; insulin is needed by the body to use sugar properly.

**epidemic:** an outbreak of a disease that spreads very fast, affecting large numbers of people in a community at the same time

**excrement:** waste matter (urine or feces) discharged from the body

**germs:** microbes or tiny particles that can cause disease

**HIV:** human immunodeficiency virus, the virus that causes AIDS in people by weakening their immune systems

**hospice:** a home-like facility providing care and support for terminally ill patients and their families

**immune:** able to resist infection and disease

**incurable:** not able to be cured

**infectious:** capable of being spread from one person to another

**lesions:** abnormal spots on areas of the body resulting from illness or injury

**lymph nodes:** small, bean-size organs of the immune system that filter lymph fluid, a clear, yellowish liquid containing water, proteins, and white blood cells

**malaria:** a disease in the tropics that gives people severe fevers and chills; it is caused by parasites in red blood cells and is transmitted by infected mosquitoes.

**multiple sclerosis:** a chronic disease of the central nervous system that may result in loss of muscular coordination and other symptoms; also known by its acronym, MS

**opportunistic infections:** diseases caused by a weakened immune system unable to fight bacteria, viruses, parasites, and other germs; also known by the acronym OIs

**oral sex:** sex in which there is contact between the mouth and the genitals

**pandemic:** a widespread epidemic that affects an entire country, continent, or the whole world at the same time

**PCP:** *pneumocystis* pneumonia, a type of pneumonia or lung disease causing severe breathing problems seen in people with weak immune systems

**primates:** a group of mammals that includes humans, apes, and monkeys

**replicate:** to make an exact copy of something

**semen:** male reproductive fluid that comes out of the penis

**Standard Precautions:** safety procedures developed for use in medical settings to prevent the spread of germs from one person to another

**stigma:** something that is considered by people to be bad, disgraceful, or not normal

**strain:** a subgroup or variation of a virus or other germ that is able to cause disease

**T cell:** a type of white blood cell important to the immune system

**thrush:** sore patches in the mouth caused by a fungus called *Candida albicans*

**thymus:** a gland in the upper chest under the breastbone in humans; it grows throughout childhood until the teenage years (puberty), after which it decreases in size.

**toxic:** relating to or caused by something poisonous

**transfusion:** the transferring of a blood solution into the vein of a person in a medical setting

**tuberculosis:** a bacterial infection that can spread to any organ in the body but is usually found in the lungs; also known as TB

**vaginal fluids:** secretions from the vagina, including menstrual blood

**viral load:** the amount of virus present in the blood of an HIV-infected person

**viruses:** tiny organisms that can reproduce themselves only when they are inside living cells

**window period:** the time from HIV infection until HIV antibodies are detectable in certain lab tests

**yellow fever:** an infectious tropical disease caused by the bite of a mosquito; its symptoms include fever, jaundice, and vomiting.

# BIBLIOGRAPHY

The tidal wave of important information about HIV/AIDS went on during the more than ten years that I worked on this book. It continues today. The sources I used for this book are by no means exhaustive, but they did help me, as a person without formal medical training, begin to grasp the complexities of HIV/AIDS in both a scientific and social sense.

I am particularly indebted to two outstanding works:

Bellenir, Karen, editor. *AIDS Sourcebook, Second Edition*. Detroit: Omnigraphics, 1999.

Smith, Raymond A., editor. *Encyclopedia of AIDS: A Social, Political, Cultural, and Scientific Record of the HIV Epidemic*. New York: Penguin, 2001.

I turned to the following book for help in understanding certain medical terms:

Somerville, Robert, project editor, et al. *The Medical Advisor: The Complete Guide to Alternative and Conventional Treatments*. Alexandria, VA: Time-Life Books, 1996.

Certain thought-provoking books were touchstones for me. They reminded me of why I needed to write this book.

Behrman, Greg. *The Invisible People: How the U.S. Has Slept Through the Global AIDS Pandemic, the Greatest Humanitarian Catastrophe of Our Time*. New York: Free Press, 2004.

Hunter, Susan. *AIDS in America.* New York: Palgrave Macmillan, 2006.

Stine, Gerald J. *AIDS Update 2001: An Annual Overview of Acquired Immune Deficiency Syndrome.* Upper Saddle River, NJ: Prentice Hall, 2001.

The following two books present matters related to sex and reproduction in a clear, concise, and commonsense way. All readers of my book who desire to know more about these things should find their way to them.

Harris, Robie H. *It's Perfectly Normal: Changing Bodies, Growing Up, Sex, and Sexual Health.* Cambridge, MA: Candlewick, 1994.

——. *It's So Amazing! A Book about Eggs, Sperm, Birth, Babies, and Families.* Cambridge, MA: Candlewick, 1999.

The experiences these dedicated doctors shared in their books about their AIDS patients gave me the courage and energy to continue working on this book:

Bayer, Ronald, and Gerald M. Oppenheimer. *AIDS Doctors: Voices from the Epidemic.* New York: Oxford University Press, 2000.

Kübler-Ross, Elisabeth. *AIDS: The Ultimate Challenge.* New York: Touchstone, 1997.

Selwyn, Peter A. *Surviving the Fall: The Personal Journey of an AIDS Doctor.* New Haven: Yale University Press, 1998.

Verghese, Abraham. *My Own Country: A Doctor's Story of a Town and Its People in the Age of AIDS*. New York: Simon & Schuster, 1994.

Stories involving people with HIV/AIDS and their caregivers were an inspiration to me at low points during both the journey our family took after Jay's diagnosis and the one I took while writing this book.

Hawkins, Anne Hunsaker. *A Small, Good Thing: Stories of Children with HIV and Those Who Care for Them*. New York: Norton, 2000.

LoGiudice, Sister Mary Ann, with Paul Grondahl. *That Place Called Home: A Very Special Love Story*. Ann Arbor: Charis, 2000.

McCarroll, Tolbert. *Childsong, Monksong: A Spiritual Journey*. New York: St. Martin's, 1994.

Wiener, Lori S., Aprille Best, and Philip A. Pizzo. *Be a Friend: Children Who Live with HIV Speak*. Morton Grove, IL: Albert Whitman, 1994.

Wolf, Bernard. *HIV Positive*. New York: Dutton Children's Books, 1997.

Two books on the subject of grief proved helpful toward the end of this project.

O'Toole, Donna. *Helping Children Grieve & Grow*. With Jerre Cory. Burnsville, NC: Compassion Books, 1998.

Worden, J. William. *Children and Grief: When a Parent Dies.* New York: Guilford, 1996.

In addition to all of the sources already listed, I consulted these excellent references for language used throughout the book and especially in the glossary.

Costello, Robert B., editor in chief. *Macmillan Dictionary for Children,* 4th rev. ed. New York: Simon & Schuster Books for Young Readers, 2001.

*DK Merriam-Webster Children's Dictionary,* rev. ed. New York: Dorling Kindersley, 2005.

Neufelt, Victoria, editor in chief. *Webster's New World College Dictionary,* 3rd ed. New York: Macmillan, 1996.

I am also indebted to so many newspapers and magazines for keeping me up-to-date on new developments relating to HIV/AIDS while this book was in progress. Of particular assistance to me in writing this book were the following three articles from the *New York Times*: "An Emblem of Crisis Made the World See the Body Anew," by Aaron Betsky, November 30, 1997; "Fast Saliva Test for H.I.V. Gains Federal Approval," by Donald G. McNeil, Jr., March 27, 2004; and "Scientists Trace Link Between Chimp Virus and H.I.V.," by Lawrence K. Altman, May 26, 2006.

Last, I found Princess Diana's remarks from a speech in April 1991 about people with HIV quoted in *LFP Presents: A Tribute to Diana, Princess of Wales,* vol. 2, no. 2, 1997.

# THANK YOU!

I am not a doctor, scientist, or medical person, so I am very grateful to my friends Jeff, who is a physician, and Susan, who is a surgical nurse, for their help with this book.

I would also like to thank the following people for their patience, encouragement, assistance, and belief in this project: Frank, Barbara, Mary Lee, James, Sheldon, Linda, Jan, Nick, Lindsay, Kelsey, Gladys, Carin, Nancy, Ann, Joyce, Beryl, Theone, Pat, Ruth, and Eileen. I could not have done this book without you or even survived the ordeals of the past decade, for that matter.

Others gave of their valuable time and expertise as the journey of this book neared its end. My special appreciation goes to John, Penni, and Bonnie, who gave me helpful and honest feedback about the content of the book.

I am also indebted to Amy Ehrlich, an editor; Hannah Mahoney, a copy editor; Lucy Oppenheimer Hickey, a grief counselor; Jan Hudis, a family counselor; Dr. David Balk, an adolescent bereavement expert; Dr. Lisa Fitzpatrick, an AIDS doctor and researcher; and Dr. Diane Havlir, an AIDS doctor and researcher. Without your expertise and careful review of this material, the book would not be in its present form. Most important of all, you gave me the courage to confront all the difficult issues surrounding HIV/AIDS in America.

And, finally, I would like to thank Karen Lotz, the editor who first believed in this book, and Andrea Tompa, the editor who continued to believe in it. You were most instrumental in pulling this project together. You both helped me overcome all kinds of obstacles while writing the book. This book exists only because of you.

# INDEX